Little Dogs of the Prairie

Little Dogs of the Prairie

words by Jack Denton Scott

photographs by Ozzie Sweet

G. P. PUTNAM'S SONS
NEW YORK

Text copyright ©1977 by Jack Denton Scott
Photographs copyright ©1977 by Ozzie Sweet
All rights reserved. Published simultaneously in Canada by Longman Canada Limited, Toronto.
Printed in the United States of America
Drawings by Pamela Sweet Distler
Designed by Bobye List

Library of Congress Cataloging in Publication Data
Scott, Jack Denton, 1915-
Little dogs of the prairie.
SUMMARY: Examines the habits and colonies of the prairie dog, a vanishing form of American wildlife.
1. Prairie dogs—Juvenile literature. [1. Prairie dogs] I. Sweet, Ozzie. II. Title.
QL737.R68S36   599'.3232   76-56217
ISBN 0-399-20561-6   ISBN 0-399-61050-2 lib. bdg.

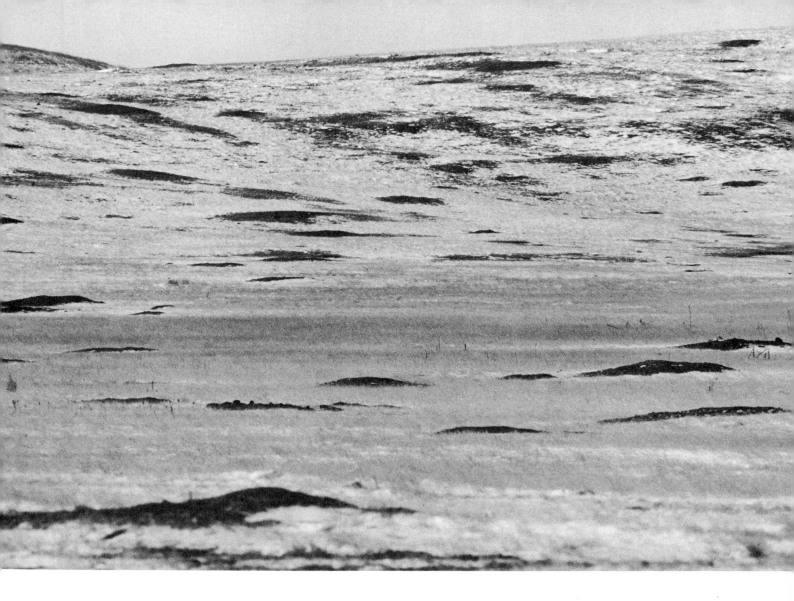

DAWN COMES ACROSS THE HORIZON OF THE
Western prairie. It flows over the flatlands, sweeping night before it,
dissolving shadows and lifting early-morning mists.

In the seeping, stalking light, the prairie resembles the eroded
bottom of the inland sea it once was eons ago after glaciers from the
north had gouged out the land. But as the sun climbs higher over the
strange-looking, spiky needle grass that has thrived on the prairie-
lands for millions of years, small craters take shape. They look as if
they have exploded out of the earth.

Blue grama grass, the most widely distributed of the prairie grasses, begins to sparkle in the foreground, and there are faint, almost imperceptible stirrings in the craters. In a curious, cautious slow motion, the crown of what could be a tiny head begins to emerge. Buff-colored, it almost blends in with the background of grass.

Now the eyes are clearly visible. Then, suddenly, as if pushed up from below, a full head pops up, sun highlighting a silvery fringe of chin and neck hair. Next the forequarters and short-eared head of a pale cinnamon animal come up from the dark hole in the prairie ground. It remains motionless, nose high, eyes alert, patiently watching, listening. The same scene is occurring in all the craters.

Now, as if by some prearranged signal when the sun is above the horizon, one of our most unique wild animals, the prairie dog, stands in full view beside each of the craters in one of America's most unusual towns, a prairie dog town.

These craters are in reality the entrances to burrows. In established prairie dog communities such as this one, there can be over fifty burrows per acre. During the last part of the 19th century sights such as this were common from Canada to Mexico, and from the Rocky Mountains to Kansas and Nebraska along the 97th and 98th meridian. Over 600,000 square miles were occupied by five billion prairie dogs. In Texas, a single megalopolis, spreading over 25,000 square miles, 100 miles wide, and 250 miles long, held an estimated 400 million prairie dog residents.

Today, the prairie dog has become another vanishing wildlife treasure, and although its numbers have not been diminished as

much as the buffalo, it is an uncommon sight for tourists and animal lovers even on the vast plains where it once was as much a part of the environment as the grass.

This dog town is in South Dakota, which leads the West in prairie dog population, with 75,000 acres of towns, and the largest collection in any single area, on the Pine Ridge Indian Reservation in the southern part of the state. Although there may be a few prairie dogs in some other states, the main concentrations of the little animals today are in the western Dakotas, Utah, Wyoming, Montana, eastern Colorado, Kansas, and western Oklahoma.

Like all of their kind, the occupants of this South Dakota town begin leaving their underground homes at sunrise and usually remain in the upper world until sunset. This adult male stands beside his burrow sometimes for as long as half an hour, letting the first rays of the sun warm him while he cautiously watches and listens to be sure that his outside world is safe before venturing out.

He is a handsome representative of the Sciuridae, or squirrel family, and is closely related to chipmunks, marmots, and ground squirrels. He is in fact a rarity, a burrowing ground squirrel, with relatives in far places—the cavies in South America, the hamsters in Asia and the wombats in Australia.

His identification is more complex than was formerly believed when he roamed the range in the millions with the buffalo. Then prairie dogs were simply divided into two classes, the black-tailed plains dog which we see here, and the white-tailed animal of the mountains. Now grouped in the subgenus Cynomys (derived from the Greek Kynos, meaning dog), the prairie dog has seven subclassifications, ranging from this black-tailed prairie dog, through the Arizona, the Mexican, the Utah, the Gunnison's, the white-tailed (in the mountains of Colorado, Montana, Wyoming, and Utah), and the Zuni. There is a slight variation in size and coloring in most of the subspecies.

A general description, however, would make all species short-legged and pudgy, with coarse but close tawny fur ranging from gray-brown to red-brown and pale cinnamon, grizzled with black, and with white undersides. They can grow as long as fifteen inches, and weigh as much as three pounds. Smaller than a woodchuck, larger than a ground squirrel, the ears are short, the head somewhat flattened, and the eyes are set high so vision overhead is keen. The tails, one fifth of the body's total length, are tipped with black, which gives this plains animal part of its name.

But history had a hand in naming this very special social animal which is seen nowhere except in North America. The Spanish explorer Francisco Coronado saw prairie dogs in 1541 when he marched from Mexico to Kansas. Even then, before it was known what they were, he intelligently compared them with squirrels.

In 1742 French explorers Louis and François Vérendrye heard the

prairie dogs bark, saw no resemblance to squirrels about them, and called them <u>petits chiens</u>, little dogs, so naming this most popular dweller of our prairies.

On their historically famous expedition opening the West, Lewis and Clark at first also called them "little dogs," but this was later changed in their journal to "barking squirrels."

Science pulled it all together in two words, <u>Cynomys ludovucianus</u>—Plains, or Black-tailed Prairie Dog—and it is as the fascinating prairie dog that we all know the animal we are watching.

As this plains dog stands by his burrow, bolder, friendly neighbors come out into the sunlight that is casting a pale golden patina over the prairie.

First comes a family of graceful, alert pronghorn antelope, gleaming amber in the morning light, their clear white rump patches like huge powder puffs. Not far from them in a rich growth of mesquite grass two wary wild turkeys carefully survey the terrain, and beyond them stands the vanquished lord of the prairie, the buffalo, who now, thanks to conscience-stricken people who have helped, is successfully making a comeback.

These animals, along with the prairie dog, cooperatively fitted into nature's scheme of ecological balance. Antelope filled a niche between the wide-roving buffalo and the mostly stay-at-home prairie dog by not competing for food with either. Antelope ate the forbs, which are herbaceous plants such as locoweed, fringed sagebrush, larkspur, yarrow, bindweed, snakeweed, and even the numerous prickly-pear cacti. Buffalo cropped the grass short, but left plenty for the prairie dog, and its close-cropping of the high grasses also aided the visibility of the prairie dog, which in turn helped the latter to survive.

As the antelope peacefully graze, the turkeys leave their cover, and the buffalo ambles onto the open grassland, the prairie dogs move away from their burrows to feed on the grass.

A sudden sound freezes them.

A high-pitched sound, almost a scream, it is a two-tone bark. An alarm call. An enemy is close.

A large male prairie dog stands erect beside his burrow, head flung toward the sky, his bark so intense that the effort sends a paroxysm through his body, ending with a violent jerking of his tail.

Overhead on silent wings is the enemy, a golden eagle.

Within seconds the dog town that was beginning to stir into morning motion is empty. Warned by that urgent barking, the prairie dogs have vanished underground.

The eagle banks slightly, catches a warm air current and rises with it, floating slowly, carefully, over the deserted burrows, looking for a straggler or for a young prairie dog that didn't heed the siren-sharp warning. Swift, silent and efficient, the eagle hangs in the sky almost motionless. Then, satisfied that nothing of interest is stirring above ground, it spreads its wings into a seven-foot fan and calmly flaps away, searching for other prey or another prairie dog town where the sentries perhaps aren't so wary.

Despite the bird's skill, hunting for prairie dogs is not easy, nor is it always successful, for a thousand eyes watch the sky from every dog town, and the alert barking sentries send all the little dogs scurrying below. The sick, the unfit, and the very old may not always react quickly enough; thus the eagle may be said to help ensure that mainly the fittest prairie dogs survive.

Those barkings are the prairie dog's strongest weapon of defense. So diverse and wide are the range of barkings that they may almost be called a song of survival.

John A. King, studying prairie dogs in Shirttail Canyon, Wind Cave National Park, South Dakota, discovered that their barks have precise meanings, and he identified some calls in the barking language.

(1) The alarm bark is two-syllabled, sounding like tic-uhl, tic-uhl, tic-uhl, the first syllable much higher and shorter than the second.

(2) The eagle or hawk, danger-in-the-sky warning bark, is more frenzied and urgent than any other. Both notes of that bark are uttered at the highest pitch the little dog can manage. When that call sounds, no matter where they are or what they are doing, all prairie dogs respond instantly. If they are caught in the open they flatten themselves on the ground, to be as unobtrusive as possible. If eating grass, they try to camouflage themselves among the blades.

Some other calls in the bark language are:

(3) The defense bark, high-pitched, repeated at intervals, uttered when a male from one territory tries to drive another animal out of it back into its own area, or when a male ventures out of his own range into another where males are absent.

(4) Muffled bark, when two females are warning other prairie dogs away from their nesting territories.

(5) Territorial call, or all-clear bark, which may be given simply to declare territorial ownership, or may be sounded to indicate that danger is past and normal activities can be resumed.

(6) The churr call, which is an evidence of displeasure or anger.

(7) Fear scream, made mostly by the young, sounding much like a baby crying.

(8) Tooth chattering, accompanied by a very low bark-growl, which is made when the little dogs are in a dispute over food or when they are annoyed if chased into their burrows.

But if the bark is the prairie dog's sound of survival, patience is the little dog's armor. After the South Dakota prairie dogs vanish into their burrows at the eagle alarm, they stay just inside their escape hatches for almost an hour, listening intently for any other warning or sound that would indicate that danger is still present. Finally, one prairie dog bravely emerges and sounds the all-clear bark, and other prairie dogs begin to appear. The general reemergence of the town from the burrows is like a slow-motion ballet in its beauty and economy of action.

Slowly, out comes that wary head with its high-set excellent eyes that can detect abnormal motion at hundreds of yards (an orange shade of color in the eye permits them to withstand even the direct glare of the sun) and the open, short ears that can pick up sounds that the ears of a human cannot. Inch by inch each prairie dog moves out of its den and stands motionless, watching and listening, all four feet firmly planted, enabling the dogs to quickly whirl and reenter the burrow if necessary.

All is quiet now, and from burrow after burrow more little dogs come out and survey the grassland sea around them before they start this day that was interrupted by danger from the sky.

It could be said that the life of the prairie dog is one of constant downs and ups, for enemies are numerous. But among those enemies and friends an entire wildlife circle is created by prairie dogs. Their vacant burrows give shelter to burrowing owls, rabbits, other ground squirrels, toads, crickets, and even snakes. The little dogs themselves are the natural prey of coyotes, wolves, badgers, black-footed ferrets (which now, because prairie dogs are a dwindling species, are considered one of the rarest mammals in North America), foxes, bobcats, blue dart and rough-legged hawks, golden eagles, and prairie rattlesnakes. Thus, this entire ecosystem was, and to some extent still is, mainly dependent upon prairie dogs. When their large populations were decimated, so was too much of the wildlife of the Great Plains.

Today, however, enough enemies are left to keep the residents of the few prairie dog towns forever on the alert.

These prairie dogs finally move from their den entrances, singly and in pairs, placidly waddling across the soft soil near their burrows into the grass for the first normal activity of their day, searching for breakfast.

They are mainly vegetarians, although they will eat insects, with grasshoppers a favorite. They will eat on all fours like other grazing animals, but they prefer to sit upright, using their dexterous paws like hands, as their squirrel relatives do. The erect position permits them to keep watch for danger as they feed. Bluestem and peppergrass are favorites, but they also relish blue grama, buffalo and tumble grass, brome, foxtail, fescue, and sand dropseeds. Their first choice is always grass, but they will eat pigweed, and they like the runners of buffalo grass stolons. They always sit upright when munching on the taller grasses such as western wheat or June grass, hold the stems in their paws, nibble off the leaves and seeds, and throw the stem away.

In fair weather the little dogs will feed until ten or eleven in the morning; on dark days they may feed from time to time throughout the entire day. Two hours before sunset they have their heartiest meal, eating the grasses from top to bottom. Some observers believe that this is a planned action, not mere appetite, for the safety of prairie dogs depends upon their vision. In high grass it would be limited and they would be vulnerable to their ground enemies. So, within 100 feet of their burrows, they cut down all grass or plants over six inches high.

They are well equipped for their grass diet; the incisors are long, the molars broad and strong. The stomach is large; the caecum even larger. According to scientists, this enables 250 prairie dogs to consume as much grass in one day as a thousand-pound cow. This large quantity of starchy food in the stomach is also converted by chemical action into water; thus prairie dogs can go for long periods without drinking.

Eating, however, is not the main occupation of these beguiling plains dwellers. Knowing that their home is not only their refuge but their lifeline, they continually keep it in good repair, cleaning out windblown soil and sand, helping one another, sometimes working singly, sometimes in pairs. Most of them are as fussy about their dens as a human housekeeper with a freshly waxed floor.

Prairie dogs are the most accomplished diggers and engineers of the burrowing animals. Coupled with their long, effective claws is what seems to be inexhaustible energy, plus the ability and the willingness to help one another with den-building chores.

Regardless of what activity is going on in a prairie dog town, sentries keep watch constantly, digging or feeding for only seconds at a time before they halt to scan the vicinity for danger. Prairie dogs that are digging inside burrows depend upon those above ground for alarm signals. It is not uncommon for a quartet of prairie dogs to stand upright like palace guards and face in four directions to watch for danger. It is not known if these animals have been selected as sentries or if they take it upon themselves to arrange such an efficient system, but this four-dog team is frequently seen, and they have been observed standing for as long as half an hour in this erect guards' attitude.

They are not only on the lookout for danger, but for other prairie dogs that are intruders in their domain. Prairie dogs are socially unique animals that do not permit outsiders, even of their own species, in their midst despite the fact that they are community dwellers.

Prairie towns are in effect many closed communities. A town may hold hundreds or even thousands of residents, but within it are intimate groups, or "neighborhoods," which all have their own defined invisible boundaries or territories established by the prairie dogs within that area. These "clans" vigilantly maintain boundary lines. This intercolony system is so highly developed that the towns often are divided into wards, then within the wards there are small subdivisions. The clans can consist of a dominant adult male, four or five adult females, and six or seven young. Or they may have thirty young, or, again, be all adults. There doesn't seem to be any precise pattern of numbers. Some observers believe that the clans are always families with grandmothers and grandfathers and all their offspring, including in-laws and their young.

One fact is certain: Each clan vigorously defends its neighborhood. Fights usually start when males leave their own areas and encroach upon another clan's territory. This territorial imperative is so highly developed that the battle begins when the clan intruders are only a foot within another's region. The contests can be fierce, with the defenders slashing the heads of the invaders with their long incisors, and the attacked interlopers fighting back with equal ferocity. No one is certain why, on occasion, some prairie dogs cross into another territory. Some observers attribute it to boredom, others to high-spirited vigor, with young adults "feeling their oats."

The clans mainly live in peace, with much sunbathing and grooming, often standing or sitting side by side with their forelegs around one another. Clan members are identified by touching noses and sometimes "kissing." Tribal in structure and manner, the clan offers complete community cooperation. The members share burrows in time of danger, help one another dig new homes, share food resources, defend one another from strangers, share sentry duties, and generally live a tranquil life of respect for one another. Fights among clan members are rare, but sometimes a dominant male will drive other prairie dogs away from choice food.

Despite food activities, fights between clans, and the constant warnings and diving into the burrows to escape danger, the focal point of the prairie dog's life is its home—its burrow—the most remarkable of that of any North American mammal. The exterior of these masterpieces of excavation is either dome-shaped or crater-shaped. The crater's conical mounds are formed of a combination of topsoil, subsoil, roots, and grass from the edge of the mound. Dome dens are round mounds of subsoil with the burrow entrance in the top.

Long hours are spent shaping mounds, with the little dogs digging soil with their front claws, kicking it back out of the tunnel, or pushing it out with their front legs. After a rain they carefully tamp the soil around the upper mounds into place. Pushing or carrying the soil to the place where it is needed at the mound, the prairie dog then, on all fours, body, neck, and head rigid, shoulders hunched, forcefully rams its nose into the soft soil, packing it tightly. What the furry little engineer is doing is creating a dike around the entrance to its burrow. Circular, one to two feet high, the soil, packed hard by that power of body and nose, prevents rainstorms from soaking the inner den.

Those den interiors are impressive feats of excavation, going below from five to fifteen feet deep; then from the bottom of that vertical shaft a tunnel can shoot off horizontally for eighty or more feet. That finished tunnel also veers upward to a cunning, hidden escape hole which the prairie dog uses when an enemy actually gets into its den.

This unusual underground home has side tunnels, a couple of bedrooms, toilet, storage room, nursery, and listening post. From the bottom of the entrance the den may again be slanted upward to about two feet below the surface. Enlarging this creates an air trap, or an area where the prairie dog can seek refuge if its burrow should be flooded.

Various biologists have engaged in the laborious task of excavating prairie dog burrows, and have found that no two are alike. Maxwell Wilcomb, Jr., exposed thirteen tunnels and determined that they varied in length from 15½ feet to 86 feet, the depth varying from 34 inches to 73 inches. He found that most burrows had a single entrance dug through a dome of earth or passing through a cratered mound. Even the listening rooms, where the prairie dog dives and waits to see if the danger is real and imminent or transitory, differ. One was a mere 20 inches inside the tunnel; another was more than 8 feet from the entrance.

These listening posts are large enough for the animal to turn around in, giving it the opportunity to head either way, for the surface or deeper underground. Some tunnels didn't have them, but all had nest chambers completely lined with grass. Wilcomb also found one case in which several prairie dogs had merged tunnels, creating an underground condominium.

These unique underground tunnels seem to be planned with precision, providing for air circulation and for flooding in case the mound dike doesn't work. A number of years ago a rancher in Texas ditched the water from a nearby lake into a prairie dog town. About three feet of water covered the entire surface of the town for half an hour. Shortly after all the water had vanished into the holes, prairie dogs started emerging from their burrows through escape hatches they had planned and opened.

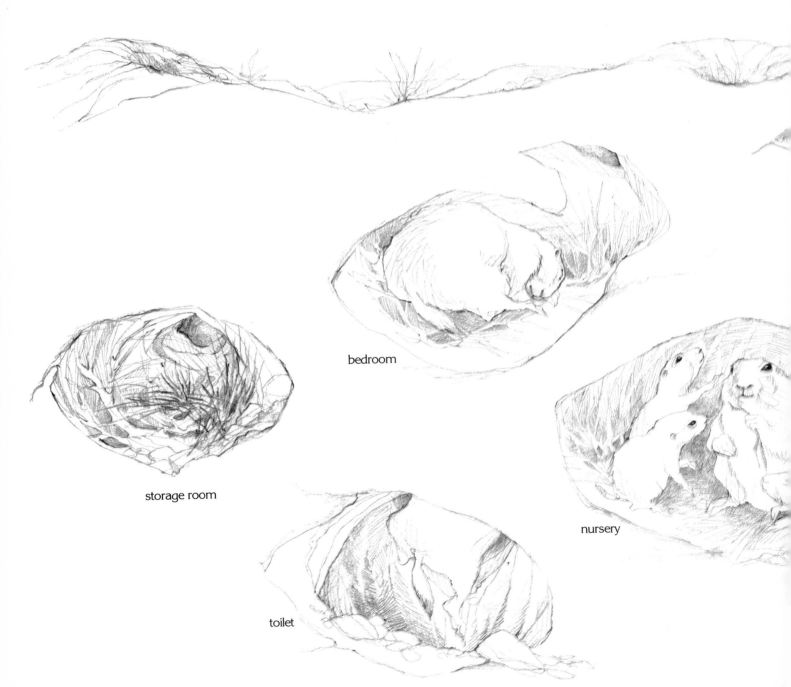

bedroom

storage room

nursery

toilet

Some naturalists believe that these burrows actually benefit the land in which they are dug. In one experiment 15,000 gallons of water were poured into a prairie dog burrow. Even that amount of water didn't fill it. The conclusion was that much of the water stored under the plains of Texas (where a huge amount continually is pumped out by wells and much of it used for irrigation) probably penetrated that hard soil of the plains by first pouring down prairie dog burrows.

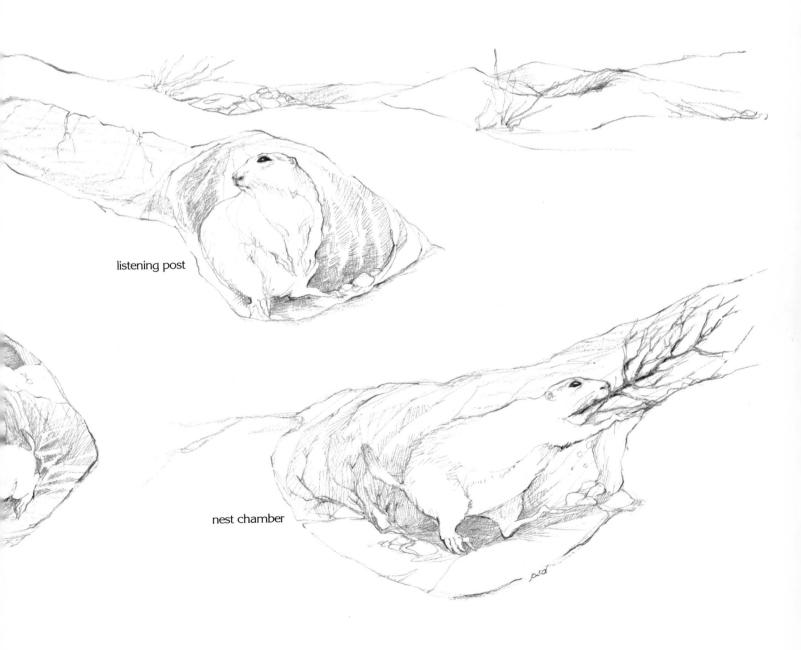

listening post

nest chamber

Despite the amount of labor needed to dig their large homes, prairie dogs do not work all the time. They also take time out to just sit and rest and look off across the prairie. But no matter what they are doing they will halt from time to time and check to see that all is well in their world. They live in fear of an enemy entering their town without a warning being sounded. It does not happen often, but it has happened. Thus the mode of life is work and watch; stop, look, listen.

If it is springtime, that lifestyle of constant watching can bring a male and a female together. An almost two-year-old, creamy cinnamon female is seen from afar by a two-year-old male who has

been ready to mate for two weeks. Females do not breed during their first year, and thereafter only once a year. This one has never mated and has been in the mating mood for only three days.

With males interested before females, in the early spring dog towns are filled with male yippings. The only sound that rises above their shrill mating calls is the strident cries of the sentries warning of danger.

Anxious-to-mate males will carelessly mark off territorial boundaries, belligerently try to "kiss" and make up to the females who, if they are not ready, will drive the males away from their burrows. At night the males will go to the winter burrows, the not-ready females to the nesting burrows. Touchy and nervous, males will often fight one another, apparently for no other reason than it is the mating season and they must prove their physical superiority.

The young male who has observed the creamy cinnamon female now approaches her, touches noses, then tries to "hug" her. If she does not permit it, he will follow her around until she is ready. If another male approaches, he drives him away; if the other male persists, a fierce fight can ensue.

The young male now courts his selected mate, standing close to her for long periods, hugging her, sometimes kissing. From that point on they are together most of the time. The nesting burrow they select may have been inherited from the female's mother and probably is roomy and well-built, having been constructed by a pair of experienced adults. Even so, after a long winter of use, it needs a thorough housecleaning, and the new pair go to work to clean it out. It doesn't involve the labor of building a new den, but it is much more than an overnight task. They work long hours, sometimes not stopping until the dying rays of sunlight begin to sparkle red on the prairie grass.

When the nest burrow is ready, the female gathers grass to line the underground chamber where her young will be born. Gestation period for those young is from twenty-eight to thirty-two days, giving her plenty of time for nest-building.

Before she carries the last of the nesting grass into the den, the female carefully puts it down and stands erect for a long period. She may be looking for her mate, or checking for danger, or perhaps she is taking a last long look around before she goes below where she will spend much of her time now. Prairie dogs take motherhood seriously. The males, however, play no part in raising the family they helped create. But they are good-natured about it and mingle with the offspring after they are weaned.

When the young are born (the litter ranging from two to ten, averaging five) in the sweet-smelling prairie grass which lines their nest, they weigh about half an ounce apiece. But they grow rapidly, in one week increasing their weight by 40 percent. In two weeks they are two and a half times their weight at birth and are covered with fine, almost golden hair. In sixteen days they make squeaking sounds, at three weeks they can stand, and at one month they crawl about the nest. At just over one month their eyes open and they can walk, then in a day or two run and make puppy barking sounds.

The next six weeks are busy ones below, the young not emerging yet but exploring their large and complicated home. During this period their mother brings them choice young grass and tempts them to eat. By the end of the seventh week they are weaned and raring to pop up and find out what their new world looks like.

When their parent feels the time is right for them to visit the upper world with its many dangers, she goes up first, carefully seeing that all is safe. Then she descends and herds her little ones along the tunnel to the entrance. They emerge hesitantly from the burrow, little pale beige bundles of timid curiosity, instinct and instruction keeping them within a few feet of the safety of the burrow entrance.

They carefully seek out the tenderest and sweetest grass, some sitting erect like their parent while eating it. They are naturally cautious and will dart for their burrow at an unexpected yip, or a shadow, or a strong wind in the grass. But at this point they are also under constant instruction. Their mother teaches them to watch and listen for danger and to recognize exactly which barks mean danger. In a short time the little pups are so adept at diving into their burrows that some of them are faster than their mother.

Like all puppies, young prairie dogs are playful and appealing, romping and rolling in the sun, mock fighting, somersaulting, leaping over one another, sitting upright, then falling over backward.

And they are pampered by all the adults in the clan, who kiss and groom them and frolic with them. Some of the older males won't play, but will hold the squirming little dogs still and carefully groom them instead.

One observer saw young prairie dogs playing what he called "their version of prisoner's base." One dog ran toward the burrow of another, while a third tried to get into the first dog's den before it could turn around and race back to its own den. "The game spread until the whole village was in wild excitement of dartings, cross-runnings and tactics of blocking and interference. The prairie dogs' whistling and squealing rose to an excited uproar like the tumult at a baseball park."

Often the young from two or three parents will gather and sit together for long periods, a few will start digging tiny trenches, and others will munch quietly on grass. Some will lead little expeditions to find greener fields.

These weaned wildlife offspring are fortunate, for before winter comes their mother will turn over the den to them while she goes off, and with the help of clan members digs herself a new home. Thus these little dogs, feeding, frolicking, and lazing in the sun, do not have to labor at all until the following spring when they may go looking for individual den sites to dig out for themselves. They may also venture into new territory, expanding their food horizons, or the parents themselves may go looking for new areas at the edge of town. But they never go far; dog towns, unless there is a catastrophe such as a continuing drought or a vanishing food supply, are fairly permanent places. One town on a ranch in Colorado has been thriving there for over fifty years.

The lusty adult male sentry is partially in his den when he barks the alarm. These South Dakota young feeding in the sunlight have been so well trained, however, that when they hear that sudden bark, two of them stand, nervously alert. One stops eating. In seconds they are underground. With this kind of alert reaction, these pups may make it through their five-year life span.

The enemy has slithered silently in, almost catching the entire neighborhood unaware. This is an enemy that can actually enter the deep burrows.

All over the neighborhood prairie dogs instantly halt activity; carefully look around for the danger crawling amidst them. Many of the adults do not dive into their dens. The bark alarm alerted them to what the danger truly is and they are prepared to do battle if they must.

For this enemy does not attack mature prairie dogs. It seeks the young.

As the original alarm bark fades, other adults take it up, some standing head tilted to the heavens; others, lying in the sunlight, simply raise their heads and yowl, echoing the alert throughout every neighborhood in the town, trying to caution even the most carefree young.

The reason for the alarm is the prairie rattlesnake. A constant visitor, sometimes a resident in dog towns, often sleeping, sometimes even hibernating, in abandoned burrows, this forty-six inch poisonous snake is not as large or as deadly as the six-foot diamondback rattlesnake which also inhabits the prairies, but it does prey on very young prairie dogs. It is said not to be feared by dog town residents as much as eagles and hawks, and observers' snake reports are conflicting. Some claim that adult prairie dogs set up an instant clamor when snakes appear, others say that the dogs aren't too alarmed because they see the snakes so often that they sound only desultory calls.

Reports on prairie dogs combining forces to bury rattlers in burrows also are contradictory. Some naturalists have claimed that it is simply legend, but there are written "I was there" reports such as that by veteran prairieman Charles Becker. He wrote in a national magazine that he saw a rattler vanish into a prairie dog burrow. Almost instantly a prairie dog popped up and frantically ran in circles around the entrance, barking loudly. In a short time twenty prairie dogs appeared, all barking. Suddenly they all began filling in the hole with soil, pressing it in with their noses, the way they dike their mounds. Theory is that the snake, buried alive, suffocates.

Literature of the prairie abounds in this discussion: Prairie dogs bury rattlesnakes; prairie dogs do not bury rattlers—they aren't even afraid of them.

Two points are fact: Students of the prairie dog have seen rattlesnakes kill and eat immature prairie dogs, and they have heard dog towns resounding with snake alarms.

But for wildlife all enemies aren't made of flesh and blood; some are composed of baking sun, of wind and rain, or snow and bitter cold. Winter has felled many a creature that a fanged foe couldn't touch.

But not prairie dogs. Their deep burrows are so well constructed that they can brave even the fiercest winter without too many problems. They do prepare for cold weather in the late fall, accelerating their food intake, putting on layers of fat that help sustain them through the frigid snowy days when they remain in their cozy burrows. They do not hibernate, and they do not store food to tide them over in case they are snowed in. The accumulation of fat seems to be able to do that.

Cold weather and snow do not deter them; blizzards and below-zero weather do. But they are often above ground during the milder winter days, touching noses with neighbors, gathering to sun themselves near the mound entrances. At times the surrounding snow seems like a sea breaking around them, the mound an island of safety. Hunger, however, will send them scampering across that snowy sea searching for grass.

One fact of life the prairie dog can always be certain of: Danger does not depend upon weather; it is always there. Winter may be the worst season, for another deadly enemy increases its activities during the cold months.

This time the warning bark of a sentry seems more like a hopeless wail than an alarm call. But it still sends town residents scampering for their burrows and makes them alertly look for the intruder. This enemy, like the rattlesnake, is one that can enter the burrows, so those underground havens are no refuge this time. In fact, this archenemy of prairie dogs preys on no other creature, and actually lives and raises its young in abandoned prairie dog dens.

Ironically, the thinning of prairie dog ranks everywhere brought this formidable foe a sort of fame. Sinuous, sinister-looking, a member of the weasel family, the black-footed ferret has now become perhaps the rarest mammal in North America, and may hold the number one position on the endangered animals' listing. Naturalists know very little about this mysterious creature; few humans have ever seen one. But biologists have observed them entering dens and emerging with dead prairie dog young. With almost contemptuous ease, the black-footed ferret also captures adult prairie dogs at the entrance to their burrows and drags them struggling down into the den to kill and devour them.

But, surprisingly, Donald K. Fortenbery, a biologist stationed in South Dakota, which has the largest population of prairie dogs, thus also black-footed ferrets, notes: "At times the prairie dogs are aggressive toward ferrets. They give chase as the ferrets run across the town, and even run alongside them and jump in front of them. This causes the ferrets to change direction. It is believed that this avoidance by the ferret does not denote fear, but only disregard for the dog, which seems bent on harassment rather than on actual combat."

The ferret does not kill indiscriminately, but there is another enemy who does.

Winter passes into spring and the prairie again becomes rich in grass and flowering plants, and the prairie dogs increase their activities. In some dog towns many residents never make it back into their burrows. They stagger back and drop dead at the entrance. They have eaten grain poisoned by humans—the deadliest enemy of all.

Cowboys and cattle ranchers have never liked the little dog of the prairies. Cowboys called their burrows "widow makers," claiming that too many horses stepped into them, injuring rider and horse. Cattlemen convinced politicians in Washington that prairie dogs were eating grasses that should be used by livestock. The official program to eliminate the prairie dog began in the late 1800s, gained momentum with systematic poisoning in the 1900s, and by the 1920s western livestock farmers, urged by government agents, were convinced that all prairie dogs must be exterminated. World War II stalled the poisoning plan, but it reappeared soon after the end of the war with an effective new poison, ''1080,'' and the little dogs' days were numbered. Are numbered.

Even today, unless the areas are specifically protected by local, state, federal government, or private decree, prairie dogs are still being poisoned.

As is too often the case, this destruction of the prairie dog was largely unnecessary mass murder of wildlife, when all that was required was a thinning out, a responsible population control.

The poisoning of prairie dogs also sets off a chain reaction of death. Coyotes, foxes, badgers, ferrets, even the birds of prey, may eat the poisoned animal and also die. Thus the entire poisoning program was not intelligently conceived, for the indiscriminate killing that results upsets the ecology of the prairie.

Later investigators claim that the finding of prairie dogs on depleted rangelands was an effect, not a cause. These animals, they assert, moved onto ranges that were already badly overgrazed by cattle and sheep. They point to evidence proving to them that the prairie dog became the target of its detractors only after people permitted the plains to be overgrazed by livestock, mostly wiping out the prairie dog's natural predators and thus disturbing the balance of nature, throwing the wildlife of the Great Plains out of equilibrium and destroying much of it.

Now, when most of the harm has been done, when the senseless slaughter has made the prairie dog a unique attraction even for residents in some western states where there used to be many more prairie dogs than people, it has ironically been proven that the little dog actually benefited the soil on the lands where it once lived.

One experienced soil researcher determined that four tons of earth were brought to the surface where prairie dog burrows numbered only twenty-five to an acre. One large mound in such an area was said to weigh 22,360 pounds. Soil thus carried to the surface breaks down into soluble forms of food for plants. Prairie dog burrows send air beneath the surface of the earth. This not only stimulates other forms of microbial life, but also mellows the soil. Further, deep layers of soil are fertilized by vegetation, droppings, and topsoil, all deposited by prairie dogs. In addition, prairie dog diggings—their dens—aid and improve water infiltration into the ground, which is necessary for the health of the soil.

JACK DENTON SCOTT, naturalist, epicure, and world traveler, has written books on a variety of subjects. His novel Elephant Grass warned that the Indian tiger would soon be extinct unless protected immediately. In Reader's Digest he also warned that the polar bear was becoming an endangered species. Today both predictions are fact. Mr. Scott has traveled around the world fourteen times, in and out of civilization, but his interest lies off the beaten track. His adventures with people and animals in wild areas were recorded in Passport to Adventure. A former war correspondent, he also wrote a column for the New York Herald Tribune which took him everywhere—from the swamps of Ceylon, where he looked for the giant lizard, to the jungles of India, where he studied the leopard and the tiger. His book The Duluth Mongoose, depicting how irate people saved a captive Indian mongoose from its decreed death, was called the "classic example of government by the people" by President Kennedy. Being avidly interested in cooking and gourmet foods, Mr. Scott has also written several best-selling cookbooks and is a member of the elite Cordon Bleu de France as a Commandeur Associé.

OZZIE SWEET, the renowned photographer, has shot nearly 1,700 covers for the nation's leading magazines. His interest began at age fourteen photographing wildlife in the Adirondacks where he was going to school. From there he went to the Art Center in Los Angeles to study sculpting. His interest in photography was more compelling, however, and he soon began to apprentice in commercial studies. To help finance his career, Ozzie acted bit parts in movies. He used this opportunity to study lighting and makeup on the sets. After military service as a photographic officer with the Army Air Corps, he worked for Newsweek in Washington, D.C. There he met many of the famous personalities he would later photograph... from Ingrid Bergman to Albert Einstein to Andrei Gromyko. Now strictly free-lance, for the past several years he has had a steady assignment photographing spring training at the major-league baseball camps in Florida. When Ozzie Sweet is not traveling on assignment, he lives in New Hampshire.